COLLABORATORS *In* CREATION

Victors Not Victims

Iona Hollins

Quantum Discovery
A LITERARY AGENCY

ISBN
978-1-961601-50-5 (Paperback)
978-1-961601-51-2 (eBook)

My teachers:
Miss Priscilla Johnson, my Sunday School and Church teacher, Mrs. Tatum, 8th grade teacher who treated me special in spite of my attitude, Mrs. Smith and Mr. Young who supported and encouraged me, and Ms. Mac, my favorite. She shared her lunch, her home, and her life. She taught me dignity and self respect and pride in the attainment of knowledge. She and I remain lifelong friends.

My family:
My Aunt Gush (my second mom) who lived next door to us when I was growing up. She kept my confidences and even threatened me when she thought I needed it. I knew better than to cross her.

My sister Duck, and my brother June Bug have been my two closest friends. They were always ready to defend me when I talked too much and got into trouble.

My younger siblings; Joseph, Willard and Joann were almost like my very own children. I was older, so we did not grow up together; but I loved them and treated them as my own. They too, have contributed to my life.

My mom, Ms. Mattie, and my husband, Austin, are my two lifelong companions. They truly are the "wind beneath my wings", and have never let me down. They can always be counted upon to defend me. They always have my back.

My children Guan, Ivan, and Mia complete my life, and give meaning to everything I do.

To each of you, I love you; and it is for you that I've written these stories.

And, first and foremost, to my loving Heavenly Father, through whom I live, and breathe and have my very being. He already knows these stories; He caused them to be, and sustained me and shepherded me through all of them. He has led me and allowed me to tell these stories. And so, to Him, the GREAT SHEPHERD of my life, I owe my life, and all that I am. To Him be praise and glory forever and ever, AMEN.

Table of Contents

*The Lord is my Shepherd; I shall not want. He maketh me to lie down in
green pastures: He leadeth me beside the still waters.
He restoreth my soul:
He leadeth me in the paths of righteousness
for HIS NAME'S SAKE.
Yea, though I walk through the valley
of the shadow of death, I will fear no evil:
For thou art with me;
Thy rod and thy staff they comfort me.
Thou prepareth a table before me
in the presence of mine enemies:
Thou anointest my head with oil;
My cup runneth over.
Surely goodness and mercy shall follow me
all the days of my life:
And I will dwell in the house of the LORD forever.*

This is my favorite Psalm. I learned it as a child, and it has always remained
with me. It has sustained me all of my life, and has been to me my personal
guarantee that God is my personal Shepherd, and as such, he guards me,
and keeps me, and can be trusted to guide me home.

FOREWORD

"HOW DO I EXPLAIN? HOW CAN I DESCRIBE?
A LOVE THAT GOES FROM EAST TO WEST,
AND RUNS AS DEEP AS IT IS WIDE?"

These are the words from one of my very favorite songs. It tells about the questions one might ask himself while trying to truly understand the depth and breadth of the love of God.

I find myself singing this song almost daily and wondering, "HOW DO I EXPLAIN"?

Philippians 1:6 says "Being confident of this very thing, that He who has begun a good work in you will perform it until the day of Jesus Christ". This confirms to me that my God has created me for a very special purpose, and that He will not stop until that purpose is accomplished. This gives me confidence. I don't think of my life's experiences as happenstance, but as purposeful.

You're kidding!! Do I really believe that all of my life's experiences were for a reason? What possible purpose could childhood truancy, poverty, and pain serve?

"I will use the words I know
to tell you what an awesome God you are,
but words are not enough,
to tell you of my love,
so listen to my heart".

How do I explain?

I can't, but listen to my heart through my LIFE STORIES.

BEGINNINGS

1800-1945

My great grandfather, Mr. Edwards.......My mother's grandfather (thought by mom to be a full blooded Cherokee Indian). Mom's mother was also named Mattie (Lee Edwards). There is no known picture of her, but she, like her father and mother were thought to be Cherokee from somewhere in Oklahoma.

Grandpa, Marshall Pittman......my mother's dad and step mother, Annie Woods Griggs, Grandpa's ancestors were thought to have been from the Florida Everglades, the Seminoles.

Uncle Bud, Clarence Pittman......Grandpa's brother, my mother's uncle, married to aunt Lula, lived next door to us. He told many stories to us about his family in the Everglades.

Top: The remaining Pittman children at a reunion in 1995. 1-the oldest, John Henry, 2-next oldest, my mother, Mattie, 3-3rd oldest, Ella, 4-next to youngest, Tommy, and 5-the youngest, Olivia.

Bottom: Doll Ann (grandpa's oldest child by Miss Hattie) and her husband Solomon Carter.

Grandpa's oldest child by Mattie Edwards, Marshall Pittman.

Grandpa's second oldest child by Mattie Edwards, John Henry Pittman

Grandpa's third oldest child by Mattie Edwards, Freddie Pittman.

Grandpa's fourth oldest child by Mattie Edwards, my mother, Mattie Julia Pittman.

Mom, our snake fighter, while living in Michigan. Her famous quote to us whenever we feared anything was, "If you're gonna live in the jungle, you'd better be the lion." She meant that, wherever you happen to be in life, be prepared to survive there. Malcolm X said, "By any means necessary". I think he meant the same thing.

LEADING CHARACTERS IN THE BEGINNING....

PAGE 2.....My great grand father, Mr. Edwards......My mother's grandfather (thought by mom to be a full blooded Cherokee Indian). Mom's mother was also named Mattie (Lee Edwards). There is no known picture of her, but she, like her father and mother were thought to be Cherokee from somewhere in Oklahoma.

Page 3.....Grandpa, Marshall Pittman.....my mother's dad and step mother, Annie Woods Griggs, Grandpa's ancestors were thought to have been from the Florida Everglades, the Seminoles.

Page 4.....Uncle Bud, Clarence Pittman.....Grandpa's brother, my mother's uncle, married to aunt Lula, lived next door to us. He told many stories to us about his family in the Everglades.

Page 5.....top.....The remaining Pittman children at a reunion in 1995. 1-the oldest, John Henry, 2-next oldest, my mother, Mattie, 3-3rd oldest, Ella, 4-next to youngest, Tommy, and 5-the youngest, Olivia.

Bottom, Doll Ann (grandpa's oldest child by Miss Hattie, and her husband Solomon Carter.

Page 6.....Grandpa's oldest child by Mattie Edwards, Marshall Pittman Jr.

Page 7.....Grandpa's second oldest child by Mattie Edwards, John Henry Pittman.

Page8.....Grandpa's third oldest child by Mattie Edwards, Freddie Pittman

Page 9.....Grandpa's fourth oldest child by Mattie Edwards, my mother, Mattie Julia Pittman.

BEGINNINGS

According to stories told to June Bug by our Uncle Bud, the Pittmans were descendants of Seminole Indians who originally lived in the swamps of Florida. Years before they had been captured, moved from their land in the great southeast and used as slaves. This never worked with them because they were unused to the harshness of that lifestyle. They had lived as a free people, taking care of the land, using of it only necessities of life. They believed it was their God given responsibility to care for the land and treasure it; and this they did. Only what was needed to sustain life was taken. The trees, land, and animals were all preserved for the generations.

With the coming of the white man, all this changed. A people who had roamed free, living off the land, were now captured and treated as animals. This was met with great resistance. Wars were fought and lost, those who were left ran into the dense swamp land and started a new life. There they were joined by many Blacks also escaping slavery. They made this their new homeland, and left the white man scrambling to find new labor.

Jeff Guinn's book, *Our Land Before We Die* offers an explanation to support oral versions told to our family by Uncle Bud for years. According to Guinn, during the years of slavery many runaway slaves joined Seminole Indians in the Florida everglades and took the 700 mile flight from persecution along side them as they were removed to Indian Territory. They never gave up their hope of one day having their own land. Up to 35 Seminole braves, 30 Seminole Negro warriors along with entire families including runaway slaves from Creek and Cherokee tribes who wanted to leave Indian territory, moved on from Florida to Louisiana to Oklahoma and beyond.

Miss Charles Emily Wilson, a 91 year old retired school teacher, and the last survivor of the Seminole Negro camp on Fort Clark in Brackettville, Texas, tells it this way. "Our people were originally from Africa. We came to America as slaves hundreds of years ago. Soon many of us chose to run away. We fled south to Florida, and there were taken in by the Seminoles". They fled south because they had heard there was freedom if they could get to "the Floridas". Small groups of slaves would escape, moving hundreds of miles south to reach St. Augustine. Here white men allowed slaves to be free, gave them tools for farming and even guns to help protect Florida from invaders. Soon, escaped slaves were pushed to move even further south to keep them safe from slave hunters.

In the years that followed more and more escaped slaves made their way to Florida. Their freedom and that of their host would not last because the American slave holders wanted their slaves back and they also wanted Florida. When the U. S. Seminole wars came in 1816-1818, and again in 1835, although fighting bravely, they were forced further into the everglades where they continued to survive. Although, almost completely wiped out, they continued fighting and did not sign a peace treaty with the United States until 1934. By this time, many Indians had been driven out and transferred to Indian Territory along with the blacks escaping slavery.

Somewhere in this story is the story of my great grandparents- parents of grandma Mattie Edwards Pittman (mother and father thought to be Cherokee), and grandpa Pittman whose dad Lycurtis Pittman lived among the Seminole in Florida.

At the ending of the Civil War, the issuing of the Emancipation Proclamation, and the establishment of the Freedmen's Bureau during the 1860's, many escaping blacks ventured out to claim their newly granted rights. The Pittmans moved northwest and discovered wherever they went that the promises of land, schools, and opportunity were often nullified by a larger law known as "States Rights" enforceable by a system of "Black Codes". Prevented from claiming their rights, they found themselves trapped by a system known as "sharecropping". This is the system into which my grandpa (Marshall Pitman) was born and lived for many years.

A life long study has left me without positive, concrete validation or answers: Where and how did grandpa Pittman and grandma Mattie Edwards meet? Was she already living in Arkansas or did grandpa really steal her from a reservation in Oklahoma? Questions I may never learn the answer to without a D N A search; and even then, could I trust our government to keep accurate records for people who were not considered human?

At any rate, grandpa continued moving from place to place, searching for the illusive "freedom" and "land" already granted to white citizens. Although census records, army registration, and social security records don't all agree, I've fixed the date of grandpa's birth to April, 1888 in Waverly, Louisiana.

From birth to age 19 there is no record of what he did or went. At 19, he settled first in Tallulah, Louisiana and married Hattie, a widow with 2 children. Later they moved on to Chicot county in the city of Louisiana, Arkansas. During the 1910 Government census he is listed as living with Hattie who has now given birth to two more girls-Lucy and Doll. According to the census records, he can read and write, although there is no indication he ever went to school. His occupation is listed as farmer-renting. This translated means sharecropping, since Blacks nor Indians were allowed to own property. Although the constitutional amendments 13th and 14th (disallowing slavery within the United States, and granting citizenship to slaves) passed in the 1860's and the 15th (granting the right to vote) had passed in the 1870's, because of "States Rights" many of these laws were not enforced, particularly if and when applied to blacks or Indians. In other words, there were no laws which a white man was bound to respect when it came to these groups.

By the 1920 census, although still living in Chicot county, Louisiana township in Arkansas, grandpa, 32, was married to Mattie Edwards who together, now had 5 children (Doll—from marriage with Hattie, Marshall, John Henry, Freddie, and Julia-my mother-Mattie). There is no picture of grandma Mattie, but the picture of her father shows a man believed to be Cherokee. Mom never met her grandmother or grandfather. It is unclear what happened to Hattie or her two children from a previous marriage or grandpa's first child with Hattie-Lucy. He is still listed as farming and only Doll and Marshall are enrolled in school-although they would be pulled out anytime to work in the fields.

By 1930, grandpa had moved to Coldwater, Arkansas, Cross county. He is still sharecropping and Aunt Doll is now married to Solomon Carter. They are living in the same house, rooms separated for privacy by a quilt.

Only Marshall 17, and John 14 can read and write, none of the children are enrolled in school. Clearly, education is not the priority.

During a cold winter day on January 1, 1936 grandma Mattie, only 38 years old, died. She woke with a terrible headache and after an unusually busy day of caring for her family, she went to lie down. She died, leaving 8 children and grandpa to mourn. Mom was 16 and the youngest child was 8.

Grandpa soon began looking for another wife to help with his family. He found a widow named Annie Woods Griggs whose husband had died leaving her to take care of 3 children. Enter my father, Ivory L. Griggs into my mom's life. I remember this grandma being cold and distant. Somehow she had the idea that she could marry a man with children and hate the children. Mom and her siblings moved away from home as soon as they could. How can this happen? I can't explain her motivation, but I accept what God says, "When your father and mother desert you, I will take you up". And, I know mom and her siblings all grew to be strong in spite of her.

After moving from Coldwater, Arkansas to Twist, Arkansas, then To Earle, Arkansas, mama was finally able to attend school enough to graduate from 8th grade. While the younger children were allowed to enroll in school the older boys had to drop out and help earn a living by working in the fields. Eight grade marked the end of public education for mom. In order to go further she would have to go to another town which had a high school for Black children. Grandpa would have none of it, so she went to work in the fields along with her brothers.

By every logical account, I should have never survived, and if survived, never lived beyond my teenage years. Study after study show the dismal impact of being conceived, born and raised in poverty, with limited parental education and involvement, segregated and poor housing, run down, inadequately funded public educational institutions, and poorly trained and paid teachers and staff. The prospects are exceedingly dismal, but as one who has lived it, I can say that a study or a thousand studies cannot or will not ever truly measure the impact of the grace of God in a human life.

There is unmeasured power in the grace of God. I'm reminded of what Max Lucado said, "The highest reward for a man's toil is not what he gets from it, but what he becomes by it." Growing up in such dire circumstances, being able to rely only on the grace of God, has taught me that my reward is not what I've gotten but what I've become. Our strength grows out of our weaknesses. I had to learn early that in life, heredity deals the hand, society makes the rules, but I, with God, could still play my own cards. I had to learn to "take captive every thought", and use it for good.

Looking back I cannot pinpoint a single moment, a specific action at which I became race conscious. But I do recall instances where my mom was ignored, or overlooked or simply forced to wait while a white person was served before she was—even though she had been next in line. I also remember vividly in one case where she simply left the items and walked out of the store. She was not big on talking, but she would walk away in an effort to preserve some semblance of dignity. I never forgot that. It taught me that I could not always say everything I wanted to say, but I could walk away and deny myself some need while asserting my right to self respect.

During later years I remember hearing about the many courageous acts of Blacks in the south and praying in my innocent, child like way, for their success and safety. It was during my 8th grade year, 1955, that Rosa Parks proved for everyone that to sit down, or simply walk away negated the need to talk. It was then I really learned about Civil Disobedience.

To be born Black in America in 1941 meant that your entire life and consciousness is defined by thousands upon thousands of indignities and slights. Jim Crow signs were everywhere,and constantly reminded you that you were less than human. Every outside source, every book and magazine, every movie, every form of media screamed out either a "little black Sambo", Steffin Fletcher or Hattie McDaniel (mammy), or worse yet, that you were invisible- simple did not exist. These all combined to create in me a rebellion against the status quo and an urgent passion to excel. It was no longer good enough to be good enough, but my passion grew to be the best. Not equal, but exceptional in every area of my life.

I began to live my life in constant pursuit of excellence and superiority. Labels such as "at risk", "low income", "welfare", "single parent home", "male role model", "low expectation", "poor parent participation", "poor self image", "divorce rates", "truancy", "angry, rejected, poor, cynical, malnourished", all referred to me. I knew every theory and every pundit-all who categorized me and those like me—and I purposely set out to make liars of them all.

I came to believe that in spite of everything, I, alone was in charge of my attitude and I, therefore chose to expect the best of me. My mother and my teachers were my true heroes. They believed in me and pushed and encouraged me to excel. They truly agreed with Marshall Le Luhan who said "If you treat a man as he is, he will remain as he is; but if you treat a man as he was meant to be, he will become a better man." They gave everything to me and were willing to give their lives to make me better. They built in me, my siblings and other black students of our segregated schools a respect for "can do", and a cohesiveness born of limited opportunity that has lasted forever.

SNAKES AlIVE

1945
AGE 4

I don't know anyone who likes snakes. They're evil; responsible for Adam and Eve's fall in Paradise. Snakes are the devil personified, at least in my opinion.

When I see a snake, I want to put distance between us. Let's face it, I'm a coward. I wasn't always like this; I've had my moments of catching frogs and crawfish.

I've even been known to fry a bird or two when June Bug managed to catch one.

But let's face it, NOBODY LIKES SNAKES!!

This misadventure began years ago during one of our trips to Michigan.

It was spring 1945 and the government was busily building houses. One group was built in North Wardell for white families and one group was being built for black families in South Wardell.

Separate but equal was the law, but there was nothing EQUAL about it.

At any rate, we still had not moved into our house. It was to be house#4, and was among the first to be completed. We'd come up with the down payment, but mom and dad were now worried about making the monthly installments.

They had heard from others that there was fruit to be picked in Michigan; so mom had been praying for rain to drown the cotton crops so they could go to Michigan and make some real money.

She had visions of paying off the house and living a decent life. That spring was unusually wet, so daily laborers made little money.

Each day mom and dad brought us to stay with Miss Willie until they finished working in the fields.

Soon dad made the decision mom had been praying for; they'd go to Michigan and make some real money!

To some, this may have seemed a cruel thing to do to children. After all, we all had to pack up and go for months, and this meant missing school.

Today, it is called truancy and is punishable by law; then it was known as "doing the best you could", and was necessary for survival.

In the beginning we went with our parents. At ages 6, 4, and 2, school was not the most important thing on their minds. For now, it was a matter of survival; school would be a concern later.

As I look back, it may have been the straw that broke the camel's back, and caused my parents eventual divorce.

For the next several years we made several trips to Michigan. To us kids, it seemed like a summer vacation. After all, we couldn't really do any work.

So, every year we'd pack a trunk with essentials, lock the house, and make the long, exciting trip to Michigan.

We moved from camp to camp; starting in Ludington and Suddens Bay where we picked cherries, then on to Barryton for bean picking.

It was during one trip to Barryton that dad landed the job on the turkey farm.

June Bug, Duck and I were so excited as we backed out of the driveway and headed down the gravel road. Waving to aunts, uncles, grandpa and neighbors we set out on our yearly crusade to make money.

The old, beat up, second hand, Chevy truck crawled down highway 61 headed to Michigan.

Highway 61 was the quaint, 2 lane, poorly maintained highway that we took all the way north to Cario, Illinois; through Illinois and on up to the Michigan coastline. This trip usually took a full day (about 12-14 hours) of travel, if we had no trouble.

We usually went every summer from July (the end of the chopping season) to September (the beginning of the picking season).

The school season was split to accommodate the farmers and the growing season. School usually began in November after picking season, and ran through May. After chopping season (May through the first of July) summer session was held.

Because of the growing season in Michigan, we missed the entire summer school session and had to catch up beginning in November.

So we managed to go to school for about 7 months of the scheduled 9 month school year. That worry came later; right now, we were too young to think about that, and too happy to be on our way to Michigan.

Every day, every year, our lives were determined by the rhythm of the seasons. Everything revolved around work; and in my dad's mind, work was the only thing that mattered.

He was determined to make a "decent" living and everybody's goals were subordinate to that.

It was summer of 1945 that I learned to really hate snakes. Up to that point, I never noticed them or gave them a thought.

Our housing in Suddens Bay was a big, tin, barn divided into small rooms for families. Our room had 5 wooden bunks nailed to the wall where we slept.

The bunks were covered with straw, which served as a mattress. At bedtime, mom covered the straw with a sheet so that we didn't sleep directly on the straw. We had no pillow or other cover because of the heat.

Summers were hot, even in Michigan! We slept quite comfortably, that is, until we saw the snakes.

June Bug, Duck and I usually played around outside or inside in the kitchen area until mom called us to eat. Mom insisted that we play close to her because woods surrounded the camp, and she was terrified of wild animals.

I was not afraid of wild animals. In fact, I never gave fear a thought, not until later.

This particular evening, mom sent Duck and me to our room to get something. It wasn't locked; there was nothing of value in there. All we had was a large trunk. It was locked because everything we had was inside.

The small room was furnished with a couple of chairs, the wooden bunk beds, and our trunk. That was it. Plates, forks, and food were locked in the cabinet in the kitchen area.

Whatever we came for was quickly forgotten as soon as we swung open the door. There on the pole, right above the bunks where we slept, was a snake!

We must have seen it at about the same time; we both let out a scream and scrambled back to mom as fast as we could go. Hearing our scream, mom met us, frantically trying to figure out what we were yelling about.

As soon as she understood, she ran to the barn, and to our room.

Snakes are supposed to be afraid of people. They use their tongues and ears to warn them that people or prey are near. Usually they'll scamper away, rather than stay and fight; this snake didn't seem to notice or care about us. At any rate, by the time mom got there, it was gone!

Well, that was it for us. Duck and I swore off sleeping in our bunks. We'd sneak in with mom or dad or even June Bug. Even now, I'm afraid of snakes.

August couldn't come soon enough. Even the shopping we did in Traverse City and Benton Harbor couldn't dull the experience we had.

As much as we loved waving goodbye in July, we were even happier to get back home in September.

During the years to come we'd see many more snakes. They never seemed to care that they'd invaded our world.

Daylight would often find mom in the kitchen; the three of us placed on top of a table, while she killed snakes. After a while, it became a daily ritual. However common it became, my paranoia of snakes has never subsided.

Mom, on the other hand, never hesitated to protect us, NOT EVEN FROM SNAKES!!!!!

THE LORD IS MY SHEPHERD; I SHALL NOT WANT.

CURIOSITY CAN KILL

1946
AGE 5

It can be deadly cold in Michigan. Of all the things I remember, I think most often of the long, cold winters and the sparkling deep snow. But winter passes and a splendid spring and summer follow.

Summer was my favorite time in Michigan. Flowers bloomed and beautiful, lush, green grass grew everywhere. How June Bug, Duck, and I loved to play outside during the summer!

We lived in a rather large, two story, weather beaten, frame house on a large turkey farm. Dad had gotten a job there after giving up making a living at home.

Long ago he had come to the conclusion that in order to make a living, he had to leave Wardell. There was simply no way to support a family, not to mention, get ahead.

Poorly educated black men usually lived by "sharecropping". That meant working from sun up till sun down for the owner of the land, and still earning only enough to feed your family.

Forty acres and a mule never really applied to black families; so few of them in Wardell owned anything except the clothes on their back and the few household items they accumulated along the way.

This was not working out for my dad, so he left, hoping to find a better life somewhere-anywhere.

Grandpa, dad, and my uncles had tried hauling and selling coal, hauling and selling scrap metal, and even hauling other farm workers for hire. Nothing proved long term or profitable enough to provide a decent living.

So every year, dad packed us up in his old, beat up truck and drove all the way to Michigan in search for work.

He had heard that there was work for everybody in Michigan, so off we went.

Sometimes he and mom picked fruit such as cherries or apples; whatever work was available at the time.

Sometimes, if it rained, very little was accomplished, and little money was saved to help us survive the winter back home.

Since dad got this job on the turkey farm, we'd lived in Michigan year round. June Bug and I started Kindergarten; and, although he was seven and I was five, neither of us had ever been to school.

For the first time we left Duck every day, sprawled out on the floor having a fit.

Summers were awesome. We'd play all day, running through the house, up and down the stairs.

The most fun of all was when we'd lay down at the top of the hill and roll over and over until we got to the bottom. We never worried about stopping because there was an eight feet fence at the bottom of the hill.

Mom and dad had warned us many times to play close to the house. We were told never to wander down the hill and firmly told to stay away from the fence.

The fence ran the entire length of the property, and stood about thirty yards from a deeply wooded area.

In our minds, all kinds of monsters lived there, but we never really worried about them because of the fence.

Our house sat at the top of this hill. It had ample front and side yard area for us to play. The trees were tall and provided cooling shade. It was a great place to play, but the hill in back and the eight feet fence fascinated us.

When mom sat outside and watched us, we played our favorite game, "Hide and Seek", under the trees. But things changed the moment she went inside.

If you really wanted to pique my curiosity, just warn me of some "imagined danger". For some reason, the forbidden is more interesting. Whatever the reason, wondering got the best of me.

I was not alone in my dare devil antics; thanks to June Bug and Duck, I had plenty of company.

Every time we knew mom was busy cooking or washing or cleaning, we'd sneak out of the house. Or we'd wait until she grew tired from watching us and went inside and made our move.

Straight to the back we'd go, lay down at the top of the hill and roll over and over all the way down to the bottom.

The fence stopped us every time, so we never worried about going too far.

Today was perfect; mom wasn't feeling well. She was expecting our baby brother, Joe, in August and by early July she was getting around slowly and complaining about the hot weather.

She stayed inside most of the time, but came out periodically to check on us. Today she was cooking and dragging around, not feeling well. PERFECT!!

Keeping one eye on her, June Bug and I decided it was perfect timing to roll down the hill. Naturally, Duck tagged along.

We were going for about the fifth time when everything changed. June Bug had just checked to make sure mom was "busy". We would roll down the hill and run all the way back up and roll down again. It was a thrill a minute!!

Our fifth time around, we got all the way down before we heard it. Loud, animal, sounds came from the woods beyond the fence.

As I looked up to see what the noises were, a big, brown, daddy bear was coming towards the fence, just a few feet from us!! I saw him first, and started yelling and screaming my heart out.

June Bug startled by my screams, started to scold me, but just as he slid into the fence, he saw the bear and started yelling also. Duck, the youngest, started crying as we all ran for our lives up the hill toward the house.

I can see mom now as she tore through the door, looking startled, wondering what all the fuss was about.

We all started to talk at the same time, all the while running past mom into the house.

One by one we told what happened. Mom sat motionless waiting for us all to have our say. We were sent to wash up and sent straight to bed for a nap.

Mom finally spoke as she put us to bed, "Remember", she said quietly, "curiosity killed the cat".

Sleep finally came, but we knew we'd have a score to settle; if not now, when our dad got home.

Curiosity didn't kill us, but it certainly taught us to listen to mom. She never had to warn us about that fence again.

August 15, 1946 finally came and we had a brand new brother. June Bug, Duck, and I had another comrade to help in our daily antics. We'd just have to wait a while!!!

HE MAKETH ME TO LIE DOWN IN GREEN PASTURES: HE LEADETH ME BESIDE STILL WATERS.

WE'LL FIX YOU
BOOKER SCOTT

1947
AGE 6

The sun was hot, maybe 85 degrees or so. The wind was blowing just enough to stir the grass and flowers. Just a perfect day; how could I know that it would end this way?

Duck and I loved cooking; making mud pies that is. Every day when we could find the time, (after all, we had school to teach, church to play, and even funerals to attend to), we'd take our dolls to the back yard and pretend to be grown up. Babies meant you were grown, so we'd take on our roles, make pies and feed our dolls.

Today was not unusual; Mom and Dad had gone to work in the fields leaving the four of us at home. We each knew exactly what to do, even the youngest, baby brother Joe.

We had a small, four room, white, weather beaten frame house. House#4, straight down the road from our grandpa's. Our whole family lived in a row, the first 5 houses in the community built by the government for poor share croppers in 1943. This, in response to the "Sharecroppers Strike" of 1939; where farmers protested poor and unfair treatment by blocking highway 61 for months.

In order to clear the highway and get farmers to move and allow traffic to go through, the government began to build housing.

After moving from place to place trying to find a place where all of us could stay together, grandpa was happy for this chance for a decent house. So, he, along with my dad and uncles were the first five to give the down payment of $20.00. The houses would sell for $800.00, with monthly payments of $10.00. What a deal for us!!

The first thing Mom and Dad did was put a fence around our house. This was meant first to keep us (the children) in and to keep the roaming dogs out. In our garden we raised practically everything we ate, from fruit to vegetables and even chickens and hogs for meat.

We each knew to stay inside the fence, let nobody in, and **NEVER PLAY WITH MATCHES**. These three rules were rules to live by.

Why I decided to cook our mud pies baffles me, even today. We'd never made a fire before, because, we knew the danger. But today, I felt compelled to "fry" my pies. Back in the kitchen, I stood on tip toes, but could not reach the matches. Not to be outdone, I pulled up a chair, climbed up, felt around on the top shelf, and *ah hah,* the matches!!

I ran out of the house, not bothering to put the chair back or close the cabinet. I ran straight to Duck and blurted out the great idea that was churning around in my head. Why not "cook" the pies, "Indian Style"?

Duck knew better than to try to change my mind. She knew how determined I was, even when I was wrong. She hesitated, but did not try to stop me as I gathered sticks to make the fire. A quick strike of the match and it was a done deal.

Uncle Booker and Aunt Lula lived next door to us and we could usually expect to find them inside. They tended to their business and didn't mess with us, because we could be pretty vicious when our parents were gone. It was no secret, June Bug, Duck and I never liked Uncle Booker. It seemed he just moved in when our "real" Uncle Bud died, so we had decided to make him pay.

Every time we caught him outside we called him "Old bald head Booker Scott", while hiding safely in our room. He hated this, but couldn't pin it on any one, so he just lived with it.

Aunt Lula had flowers everywhere. She **would** pick **this** day and **this** time to water them. Old Booker must have been hiding in the house, not wanting to see us.

The fire was going great, our mud pies were cooking, but suddenly we noticed it was moving beyond our "Indian stick pile" and racing along the grass in the back yard. Both Duck and I noticed and screamed at the same time. Not to panic, June Bug, our resident fireman, grabbed some water from mama's wash tub and attempted to extinguish the fire. Seemingly, the breeze had picked up and the fire continued to swirl out of control, circling our small house.

By now we all had panicked, even Joe began to cry. Aunt Lula and Uncle Booker both heard the uproar at about the same time and came running over to our yard. They came with buckets and rugs, working feverously, until every single blaze of fire was gone.

As they finished, they turned to scold us, but noticing us frantic with worry and crying, they simply walked away.

Within minutes Mom and Dad came up. Running down the road, they ran to us yelling and screaming words I could not understand. What? How? When? Are you o k? Questions, too many to hear, too many to deal with.

Looking round, the grass was now gone, burned to a crispy, black straw. Though it was still smoking in spots, the fire was out and our house was spared. Aunt Lula and Uncle Booker had managed to put it out only feet from our house! How could we? How did we?

I remember Dad fussing, while Mom cried and held us closely. Somehow we managed to piece together the story. Placing us safely inside the house, they went next door to get the real story. We sat, still crying, fearing our punishment.

Slowly they entered the house looking tired and weary. "How many times have I told you **NOT** to play with matches"? That's all Dad said, but his look told us that the matter was far from being settled.

Waiting was the hard part. But in the meantime, Aunt Lula and Uncle Booker became very dear to us. Not only did they save our house, but somehow they saved us; at least for the moment!!

"YEA, THOUGH I WALK THROUGH THE VALLEY OF THE SHADOW OF DEATH, I WILL FEAR NO EVIL; FOR THOU ART WITH ME."

A THOUSAND
TIMES

1949
AGE 8

"If I told you one time, I've told you a thousand times. One day you'll learn to listen"

How I hated it when Mom gave that sermon. Today was the one day that she'd told us about "a thousand times". There would be no need to use that sermon with me ever again!

It started as every school day. We left for school at 7:30 and walked and played our way down the long, winding, gravel, country road to school. My brother, June Bug (2 years older), myself, and my younger sister, Duck walked together.

Other groups of kids straggled along, some ahead, some behind, all going the same place. Today it was cloudy and cold. Not that it mattered, even if it rained we still had no choice.

There was no staying home in our house. If you were breathing, you went to school.

As we walked, June Bug chided us to keep up. Every day, the same thing. We never walked fast enough for him. What he really wanted was to leave us and walk with his friends ahead, but we'd fuss and cry—whatever it took—to make him drag along with us.

To get back, he told us stories of ghosts walking around in the cemetery. He knew we'd keep close to him because we had to pass it going to school.

We always knew that an old white couple lived beyond the cemetery, way back into the woods.

We'd been warned "a thousand times" to stay away from them and leave their pecans alone.

A thousand times couldn't do for us what Old Bill did that morning.

We'd walked and skipped and run and played and sang a full 20 minutes by the time we came to the turn by the graveyard. We kept close, but were beginning to fall behind.

Just at the graveyard, June Bug and his friends ran about a third of the way in daring us to follow.

Just a few more yards would take us smack into Old Bill's pecan patch, and we all knew that meant trouble.

Looking down and stepping carefully we anxiously avoided the graves. My heart beat so loudly, I was sure I'd wake the dead. Just ahead of us the boys were busily picking up pecans when we suddenly heard what sounded like an explosion.

We all screamed and ran for our lives as we saw Old Bill running from his shack carrying his old beat up shot gun.

I never knew how fast I could run and jump, only that within minutes we were clear of the graveyard and rounding the curve toward the old bridge leading to town and the white school. One by one we ran screaming onto the bridge, running for our lives!

This bridge, built somewhere around the beginning of the century, was an old, rickety, wooden bridge with tall rusty iron banisters. It was quite narrow, barely wide enough for passing cars. It seemed unsteady, even when we walked across on our way to school. I can't imagine how it held two cars at the same time.

Wardell, with a population of 400, a couple grocery stores, a post office, and gas station had few resources for revenues to make needed repairs. Year after year there would be talk of repairs, but they never came.

Today was different, because for the first time, the school bus passed us as we ran along on the bridge. Normally we crossed before the bus, or waited for the bus to pass, but not today. We paid no attention to the bus, we were running for our lives!!

As the bus passed, we heard the usual insults yelled from the windows-____ "Get out of the way N____, we'll run over you"!! Those threats, however real they might have been, paled in comparison to the real bullets we heard in the distance.

At eight I wasn't sure what the problem was. Maybe we were taking too much space walking, maybe there was only one bus, maybe someday we could ride a bus to our school, but not today.

Today, and for many days more, we would walk to school; passing the white school, cutting through town, to go to the four room school on the southern end of town, reserved for Black children. It was 1949, and the Supreme Court would not strike down the "Separate, but Equal" law for 5 years.

We walked, we grew strong, and we learned of our ancestors and that knowledge lit a fire that would never go out. Had the Supreme Court really known, schools would have been integrated years before.

Over the bridge and a few more yards and we were completely out of hearing range. Old Bill gave up and went back inside, and the bus load of kids went into their school. We only had to walk another 30 minutes and we'd be safe at our school too!

And as for the sermon of "a thousand times", I never had to hear that sermon from mom again.

THOU PREPAREST A TABLE BEFORE ME IN THE PRESENCE OF MINE ENEMIES: THOU ANOINTEST MY HEAD WITH OIL; MY CUP RUNNETH OVER.

DIVORCE

1952
AGE 11

OUR FAMILY…..

1. June Bug (Ivory Jr.), the oldest, my very best friend. I always competed with him, and reluctantly followed his leadership—most of the time.
2. *Joseph, the 3rd youngest, the only one born in Michigan.*
3. *Duck (Mattye), the 3rd oldest, my next best friend. We often entered into coalitions against June Bug, but, they fell apart because I was chicken. Not Duck, she would fight her battles and mine too.*
4. *Me (Charlie Brown-Iona), the 2nd oldest. Duck and I are standing with Mom in front of Number 4, our house since 1944.*
5. *Butt-Nutt (Willard), our baby boy, our sweet heart, even to this day.*
6. *Joann, the youngest and smartest of the crew.*
7. *Willard and Joann as babies. They were so close, we thought of them as one, our babies.*

MOM as she appears today at 88. She still has plenty of fire in her bones. DAD as he appeared in 1979. He had remarried by then. He is sitting with my husband and son.

June Bug (Ivory, Jr.), the oldest

Joseph, the 3rd youngest, the only one born in Michigan

Butt-Nutt
(Willard, our baby boy)

Joann, the youngest

Willard and Joann as
babies

Me (Charlie Brown-Iona), Duck
(Mattye)

MOM as she appears today at 88. She still has plenty of fire in her bones.

DAD as he appeared in 1979. He had remarried by then. He is sitting with my husband and son.

I hate divorce. Marriage is meant to last "till death do us part". That's my opinion, and I'm sticking to it. But, sometimes life happens, and you simply can't fix it.

As a child growing up, I never envisioned my parents breaking up. Mom and Dad fussed and fought, but they made up, at least I thought they did.

My Dad obsessed with making a living. He never thought about the quality of life, just about making a living. He was a Christian man, living by Christian values, as far as I knew. We spent our lives working, going to school and going to church.

He was a leader in our local congregation and spent his spare time talking to people about the church. Mom was supportive as far as I could see. She made sure we had our Sunday School lessons done, and that we were ready for church on Sundays.

Growing up I remember a couple of loud fights with Dad pushing Mom, or holding her down while she tried to fight back. One fight in Michigan was because Mom spent too much for our school clothes. I remember Dad yelling, but she refused to take them back.

Mom delighted in giving us pretty, frilly, dresses. They weren't many or costly, but we were thrilled to go to school in November wearing our "new clothes".

The biggest fight happened on a cold day in January, 1952. I remember it as if it were yesterday.

During the winter months, long after the picking season ended, there would often be cotton still left in the fields. My Dad and other men who had no other work would go out and pull the rest off the stalks.

This particular winter, there was still cotton left in January. Dad knew of a place where we could all go and work for a couple of days to make some extra money.

June Bug was now 12, I was 10, Duck was 8 and Joseph was 5. Duck and Joe could go on to school, but Dad wanted June Bug and me to go with him. Mom would have none of it.

The shouting started. Mom felt that we had already missed enough school since we'd just come from Michigan in September. This meant that we'd already missed the entire summer session which we had to make up. She fiercely defended our precious time in school.

Mom had been able to complete the eight grade, but because there was no high school for black children in Earle, Arkansas she was unable to go any further in school.

This hurt her badly, but she accepted it. She swore that would never happen to her children.

I can still hear her telling us about the importance of school. When Dad wasn't talking about work, Mom was talking about school!

Do we ever get beyond the hurts that define us?

Even though Dad had dropped out of school at the end of fifth grade to "help earn a living", it didn't seem to upset him too badly. His obsession was work, not school.

So this morning, just as on other mornings, they fought about school.

There was something different. I'd never heard this language, nor seen this viciousness in Dad before. They fussed and fought, sometimes on a daily basis; but never like today.

Dad was a big man, over 6 feet tall.

Mom, on the other hand, was tiny-only 5 feet tall. She was such a beautiful woman. She often wore her hair down, where it hung almost to her waist. Her cheekbones were high, and freckles dotted her beautiful brown face. We were told that she was the spitting image of her mother which died when she was just 16.

Dad was jealous of her, and made her crazy with accusations.

At any rate, he was so much bigger than she, it was easy for him to push her around. She never took it from him, but tried to fight back as best she could.

As they fought today, Dad pushed her onto the sofa. She was fussing and crying; trying to get up. This was impossible because of his size.

Duck and I jumped on his back, trying to pull him off. We pulled, we cried, we hit; all to no avail. Only when he felt that he'd humiliated her enough did he let her up.

Jumping up, he simply walked out the door, as all of us stood crying with Mom.

Sometimes when children go to school, it would be better for them to stay home. But, Mom insisted that we go on, and not miss school. I can't imagine hearing anything the teacher said, not to mention learning anything that day.

By now, June Bug was one grade ahead of me. When we started in Michigan, we were both put in Kindergarten, but when we came back home the next year, I was kept in first grade, while June Bug was put in second.

I did not understand it at the time, but, in Michigan when we started to school, we rode the same bus that the farmer's children rode—that is, Black and white children rode the same bus and went to the same school. I never thought about it until we were back home in Wardell and had to walk to our segregated school while the white children rode a bus to their segregated school.

SEPARATE BUT EQUAL—-that was the law of the land, and we lived with it daily. Everything was separate. But, there was NOTHING equal about it!!

Every where you went there were reminders that you were separate, and NOT EQUAL. In the bus or train stations, there were separate entrances, in the court houses and other public places there were separate restrooms and drinking fountains. There was no way to rent a room in a hotel, or eat in a public restaurant (unless you were willing to go to the back door to pick up the food), and you were constantly at the mercy of the JIM CROW LAWS of the south.

This was years before Rosa Parks refused to move to the back of the bus and the massive civil rights demonstrations which eventually led to changes throughout the United States.

Our school was a small wooden building composed of several rooms which housed several grades in one room. I don't remember having playground equipment, a lunch room or any of the things one would normally expect in an elementary school.. This passed for EQUAL education as compared to the white school, which was a large brick building, with a large playground and cafeteria. And, while they rode a bus to school in winter, we wrapped up in our warmest clothes and walked or ran right past their school to our school about three miles from our home.

But we didn't know any better, or have anything to compare it with—that is—until Michigan.

By the time I was in fourth or fifth grade, we were given a bus to ride to school and no longer had to walk.

So, at Mom's insistence, we washed our face, grabbed our lunch and ran off to catch the bus.

Mom spent the day straightening up and trying to figure out what had gone so wrong.

Finally, we got home from school. We ran straight home looking for Mom.

I'm not sure what we were expecting, but Dad was not home and had been gone all day. It was not clear to Mom if he had gone to work or was just somewhere cooling off.

We ate and completed our homework by the time Dad came home. Still sulking, we knew to stay out of his way. Dad was normally good natured. He loved making jokes and was very popular with everybody.

Mom, on the other hand, was serious. She didn't kid around and had very few friends; although she was very close to her brothers and sisters. She never worried about what people said or thought. She just went about her business working and taking care of us. Even after a full, hard day's work she would often come outside and play with Duck and me. Sometimes we jumped rope, or sometimes we just sat around outside and talked.

Another argument started. What was said or done; or what precipitated it, I don't know. I only know that Mom took all of us with her to the back room and locked us all inside. Dad could be heard pacing outside the room. I don't remember sleeping, but I do remember Mom crying.

The next day was Saturday. We came out and ate. Dad had gotten his breakfast, and so, as we sat he gave us the news. He had decided to leave. He would go to Omaha, Nebraska and find work.

We screamed and cried, but he packed a small bag and walked out the door. I still remember standing in the window crying. I could not believe he was really gone. I stood and watched with my own eyes as he walked down the road toward Wardell. He stared straight ahead, not daring to look back.

In Wardell, he caught a ride to Portageville where he caught the bus to Omaha.

I actually thought I would die from heart ache. How could your own Dad walk away without even looking back? All day I sat in the window and cried. I refused to eat or drink. I simply did not believe that he was gone.

Any moment I expected him to come back down the road wearing his broad smile and announce that he was only kidding. It didn't happen, and finally when it was pitch black, and I could see nothing outside, I gave up and went to bed, still crying.

How do you comfort a hurting child?

What words can ease the pain and reassure a child that things will work out?

Mom talked her heart out trying to tell us that things would be o. k. How did she know? How could she tell? All I knew for certain was that my world had fallen apart!

June Bug grew sullen. He suddenly carried the world's biggest chip on his shoulder. Duck was hardened. She was Dad's special little girl, now he was gone. She was simply heart broken. Joe, being the youngest of four, had no idea. He just cried when we cried; otherwise he went about his business of playing.

I believe I was more hurt than anyone. I cried for days and ate only part of the time. Nothing seemed right now. How could I live if my Daddy was gone?

In a child's eyes, parents are the world. They represent everything of importance in their lives. Couldn't my Dad see that?

When divorce happens, it's like a death. I often think that death is easier, for at least, you don't have to explain it.

Explaining to others was the hardest. Back at school, kids whispered and teachers asked questions. How did I know? How could I explain?

Divorce was very uncommon in 1952. In fact, when Mom got the papers a couple of years later, we still could not understand or explain what happened or why? Divorce was not discussed and I didn't even know what the word meant, only that my Dad was gone.

If going to school was difficult, going to church was impossible. After all, Dad had been one of the leaders. How could we explain what had happened? Without even knowing the circumstances, some of the "righteous" began to whisper and put the blame squarely on Mom.

I learned years later that this was largely due to my paternal grandmother's vicious lies.

For a while, Mom would not go to church. She was so hurt and disappointed, and frankly didn't know where to turn. Thanks to grandpa, we managed to make it until chopping season.

Mom had been going to the doctor often, which was very unusual. We never went to the doctor except for emergencies. Mom prided herself on being a pretty good "witch doctor". She knew so many remedies and concoctions that visiting the doctor was extremely rare.

She never complained, or mentioned to us that she had a problem. We just knew she went to see the doctor. Finally we were told by an aunt that she had been hemorrhaging.

It seems that the day Dad left he had managed to hurt her seriously. She was bleeding heavily and about to lose the baby. We knew nothing of this; only that she was sick often and went to the doctor every week or so.

During this very difficult time, our aunts, uncles, and grandpa helped care for us. Sometimes we ate at our aunts and sometimes Mom cooked.

During the chopping season both June Bug and I joined Mom in the field. Work was more important than ever now that we had lost our Dad.

On October 18, our brother Willard was born. He was delivered by Dr. Shirey in the Hayti clinic. Dr. Shirey had been our family doctor for years and had cared for my Dad when he had pneumonia. He now urged Mom to pursue justice by charging Dad with injuring her and the baby.

It turned out that Willard had no hearing in one ear and would stutter for the rest of his life. Even armed with these facts, Mom would not turn against Dad, and refused to press charges against him.

Sometime during the next year, Dad came; not to see us, but his mother. We ran down to see him, elated at his visit. He and Mom spent time together; they talked and tried to work things out. As far as I could see, nothing changed.

He had been in Omaha about a year now and had found a job working with the state highway department. He wanted us to come and live with him, but Mom was reluctant.

Mom had heard stories about how people suffered in the city. She had been born and bred in the country. She knew how to survive there, and her family was close in case she needed help. Memories of yearly trips to Michigan were also still fresh in her mind. She imagined what would happen to us if we all gave up our home in Wardell and went to Omaha and Dad left again.

After weighing everything carefully, she refused to go.

Did Mom and Dad still care for each other? Can you be married for fourteen years and hate each other?

In 1996 during June Bug's illness, I'd finally get the answer.

Dad and Mom still cared for each other!! In spite of that, I knew in my heart that they'd never live together as husband and wife again.

That fall, Joann was born. We had settled once again into our routine of working during the harvest and going to school during school time.

By now Joseph was in school and Mom kept busy taking care of the kids, hogs and chickens, growing a garden, canning and working part time in Aunt Doll's cafe'.

We missed Dad, but life went on and we learned to live with the hand we were dealt. We learned hard lessons about life which continue to serve us.

In 1953 Dad sent the divorce papers to Mom. He asked her to sign then and return them to him quickly.

Could he really expect her to know those words or to be able to read the decree? She signed the papers, not even understanding what, or if, there were charges against her. Dad was officially out of our lives.

That never changed. He remarried, and he never made any attempt to develop a relationship with any of us.

Dad died November 30, 2000; but I have never been able to see him and Mom as divorced. I just know for sure that he is dead; as he has been to me for years!!

Do we ever get over the hurts that define us? We do. I have been shaped by the hurts of early years, but they have prepared me for a greater life I was called to live!!

I have come to agree with Helen Keller who said, "I thank God for my handicaps, for through them I have found myself, my work, and my God."

SURELY GOODNESS AND MERCY SHALL FOLLOW ME ALL THE DAYS OF MY LIFE, AND I WILL DWELL IN THE HOUSE OF THE LORD FOREVER.

OLD MAN PITTMAN

1955-1973
AGES 14-32

Grandpa sitting with Uncle C (Tommy-his youngest son) in November 1969.

My grandpa was my real life, personal hero. He was a major influence in my life. He was a small man by today's standards; only five feet seven inches and one hundred fifty pounds, soaking wet, clothes and all. But he was the wisest, kindest, strongest, most loving person in the whole world.

Grandpa was always old. I don't remember when he didn't have gray hair. OLD MAN PITTMAN was what everybody called him. To his face, however, he was Mr. Pittman.

The kids loved to tease us about grandpa. They'd say things about how he used trickery to get workers, and how he used workers to make a living for himself. In teasing they'd say, no matter what you asked him, he'd never answer you directly; he'd only said, "just get on the bus".

Grandpa and Uncle John made a living by hauling day laborers to the fields to do chopping or picking during cotton season. They would go around and get contracts with the big farmers in the area to provide workers to work their crops. It was very much like what my dad had done years earlier to make a living in Michigan.

Dad was gone now, and another man had taken his place as the most important in my life——my grandpa.

I remember most vividly his long braid. He shaved his head on both sides and wore a long braid which came down his back to his waist. His ruddy complexion was lined with large wrinkles from years of hard work and worry. His small hands were rough with large protruding veins from years of heavy lifting and straining.

Grandpa didn't have the luxury of an education. In those days, Black nor Indian men were allowed to go to school; so he taught himself to read and do rudimentary math. He could count money better than I, for it was very important to know if you were being cheated.

Not that it mattered; there was nothing you could do. Your word and your fingers meant nothing to the white owner of the store. He was free to charge anything he wanted. All you could do was complain or never shop in that store again. It was all so futile, there was no work except farm work, and no stores but their stores.

Yet, he kept a careful record of wrongs. As soon as he could, he'd move on, run away, and find somewhere else to go. He wanted his own job, his own place, his own will——his freedom.

To this day, I don't know how he learned to read.

My earliest memories of him are of times when we sat together under the big Oak tree, in the swing, reading the Bible.

This was his favorite book and now I understand why.

In wintertime, the big rocking chair in the living room was our favorite spot. To this day, when I have a problem, or when I'm stressed, I go to my favorite spot, the rocking chair. Right beside the chair, you'll find my Bible.

Each day around noon I'd find my way down the road to house #1. Years before, grandpa had seen to it that his family, my mom included, had bought houses right together in this community.

"The first five houses belong to OLD MAN PITTMAN", kids used to say. Never mind that each house had an entire family living under its roof.

To just about everybody, OLD MAN PITTMAN owned just about everything.

Grandpa had earned this reputation because whenever neighbors needed something; a ride to town, money for food or medicine, or spiritual advice, they came to grandpa. In addition, he had built up a business and was well known in the community for hauling workers to the fields or hauling coal in winter.

Grandpa was always working!!

Looking back, he was the strongest person we all knew. His children respected him with a kind of reverence.

To us he could do no wrong. And so, every day, school or not, I'd take my daily trek down to grandpa's.

Every day was a new adventure. Some days we sat in the swing and read the Bible; some days we just talked. Some days we'd go to the garden and pick cucumbers and tomatoes to eat with salt or strawberries or grapes. At harvest time, there were pails of pecans to pick up and take inside, peanuts and sweet potatoes to dig and lay out to dry, greens to pick and wash. And always, there were chickens to talk to and feed, and eggs to gather. No, this was not a farm, but I didn't know that, or care.

All I cared about was that I was with my grandpa. To me it was the best, most alive place in the world.

There were times when he'd let me help build a room in the garage, or fix the car (I watched and passed the tools). There were special times when he taught me, alone, of all his grand children, only I was taught to drive his car.

Social Science only now recognize a woman's worth. I knew then that I could do anything as well as anyone, and maybe better than most. EXCEPT GRANDPA!

Before I knew it, I'd slipped into young adulthood, and our friendship continued to grow.

On our afternoon drives, I'd share my latest "boyfriend episode", and he'd tell me about the latest "sweet young thing" he'd been thinking about. As I look back, I seriously think he was leading me on, joking, prodding me, trying to keep me talking. After all, grandpa was about 65 at the time. How could he be thinking of "sweet young things"?

More than anything else, grandpa wanted us to be "good", that is, Christian and educated. I always knew I'd go to college if grandpa had to sell the house to get me there.

There was never a question of if, only when and where.

Christianity was so important that he, along with my father, invited the church to set up a tent in our front yard for the purpose of carrying on a "revival" meeting. It was hoped that we could attract some in our community to share our faith.

As far back as I can remember, we all went to church every Sunday and carried whoever we could with us. It was very important to study the Bible and share our faith.

My father and grandpa carried on the work, along with a few other faithful men.

In the church, women sat with the children and only the men participated in a public way. Bible reading and prayer were the foundations of our worship service. That was why it was imperative that grandpa learned to read his Bible.

There was never a question of what faith I'd have, or how deep that faith would be. Even my parent's divorce didn't weaken my faith.

Leaving home, going away to college was traumatic. I'd always thought I'd be glad to "escape" the extended family syndrome. After all, there had never been an opportunity to do anything "crazy". If one relative didn't see you, another one did!!

The idea of freedom intrigued me. I'd often compared my life to that of slaves. I HAD NO FREEDOM, SO I WASN'T FREE! I had no space of my own; there was always someone to invade my privacy.

I thought going away to school would be a ball. I'd be free to be my own woman!

But how much freedom can you really have when your oldest brother also lives on campus and insists on walking you to breakfast, lunch, and dinner? At any rate, I soon discovered that I still was not free.

Little did I know, but, I'd spend the next 25 years of my life learning about freedom.

Grandpa was always the first one to get to the house when I came home from school. It meant rehashing everything I'd done since I left the last time. We'd always go shopping for something special to take back, and for "driver training" in his car.

It was more than a homecoming; it was like breathing for the first time, coming alive, being wound up and prepared to go back and be brave.

When you are one of only two in the entire family to get a chance for an education, you don't BLOW IT. You follow through, no matter the personal cost.

The phone call I dreaded did come. Grandpa had suffered a stroke. His speech, hearing, and mobility had been impaired. With one call, our entire world was crushed.

Instead of smiles and laughter, there were tears and hesitation. His eyes, filled with tears, spoke of deep pain. Our walks were interrupted by a limp and use of a cane. No more reading the Bible or talking; for him, only tears. Even when I read to him he could not hear, so he cried.

Illness shatters a world in a way nothing else can. A body once active, now incapacitated; once verbal, now silenced. Time and space once full of laughter, now full of tears. Illness is cruel, as it snaps the spirit and seeps the pride.

DEATH SOMETIMES COMES AS A FRIEND.

By the time Grandpa died, I had been married to my high school sweetheart 10 years. I had finished college and had been teaching since 1964, thus I had kept my promise to grandpa. He was so proud and every time I went home to visit I simply wallowed in that pride. Both my husband and myself were firmly established in our careers and living far from home in Chicago.

I had finally become free. I was over 500 miles from home and family, and no longer subject to their constant influence, corrections and criticisms. We were all split up—my best friend and brother, June Bug lived in Denver after serving in the Air Force and was now attending Law school, and Duck, my other best friend, was now married and living in St. Louis, while Mom and my other 3 younger siblings still lived in our house in Wardell. SO I WAS FREE! But, I was so lonely and miserable that some days I thought I would die. "BE CAREF UL WHAT YOU WISH FOR".

Now that grandpa was gone, it became my mission to help mom and my younger siblings still at home and in school. Although they still worked in the fields when school was out, there were so many needs that they never had enough money, and there were no jobs anywhere for black people in the Bootheel. School for some families was practically an option and many children still worked in the fields instead of going to school in order to meet family needs. But Mom would have none of it, it was school even if there was no food or lights.

Believing that education was indeed the key to a better life, everyone of us had left home right after graduation to attend Lincoln University in

Jefferson City, Missouri. It was the only college in the state which would accept black students. All but 1 of our family attended Lincoln, using scholarships and student work, making the best of the situation– 3 of the 6 in our family graduated from there. Myself, Duck and Joseph graduated from other colleges in other cities. FAITH IS THE SUBSTANCE OF THINGS NOT SEEN...BUT KNOWN IN THE HEART.

In spite of everything that happened in my life; the poverty, oppression, racism, and divorce of my parents, I am not a statistic. The memories are fading now, the pain is lessening. but my faith in God is greater and bolder than it has ever been. I can see clearer now why James says, "Consider it pure joy whenever you face trials. Because you know that the testing of your faith develops perseverance. Perseverance must finish its work so that you may be mature." James 1:2-4. Through this painful process I've matured and become closer to the person God created me to be.

Following is a listing of resources I've found helpful in attempting to trace my ancestry. Records are notoriously incomplete, incorrect, and/or missing altogether. But, in absence of the complete record I want, I accept what I have been able to find. My search though incomplete and imperfect is continuing.

Four Generation Chart from St. Louis County Library U.S. Census Charts from 1910, 1920, and 1930 U.S. Service Registration card from June 1917 Application For Account Number (U. S. Social Security Act) dated December 30, 1938 Plant a Family Tree published by the U. S. Postal Service (To get you Started on your own research).

NO CRYSTAL STAIR

June Bug and Joseph standing outside the tin barn where we lived while picking cherries and other fruit in Michigan. This was probably taken the summer after our Indian fire.

The old wooden bridge leading to the "white school" which can be seen to the left of the bridge.

What remained in 2000 of the "black school" located about 1 mile west of town. We had no appreciation of what Hodgen elementary school lacked in terms of teachers or supplies. It was all we had and we made the best of it

This is what remained in 2000 of our high school (Hayti Central) in Hayti, Missouri. It was the only school accepting black students in Pemiscot county where I grew up in 1955. I fmished in 1959 and won several scholarships to Lincoln University. Segregated? Inadequate? Underfunded? YES, but we made the best of what we had.

Mom, Joe and Aunt Gush in front of our home-house#4 in Wardell.

My husband of 47 years and myself.

Mom with me and my two sons. We all spend Christmas together every year we can. This has been a ritual spanning almost 50 years.

Mom with Duck, Joann, my husband and myself

Mom, Aunt Gush, myself and my husband together again at Christmas.

Mom with many of her children and grand children together at Christmas.

Seated: Ella (Pittman) Hayes and Mattie (Pittman) Griggs, standing up front: Mia Hollis, Iona (Griggs) Hollis and Mattie (Griggs) standing in the back:
Jean (mother of Lisa Hollis), Lisa Hollis (wife of Guan Hollis), Austin Hollis, Willard Griggs and Joseph Griggs. 7/2004
Here is a well-known family from Wardell, MO. Mattie (Pittman) Griggs and her sister who lived next door, Ella (Pittman) Hayes. They have a brother, John Henry Pittman, who lived down the road just south of the housing community. And their dad and mother lived in the first house on the left as you entered the housing community of Homestown, MO.
Ivory, Iona, Mattie, Willard and Joann all went to Lincoln University and graduated. If you are wondering what inspired/motives them folks to go to school, wonder no more, it was Mrs. Mattie Griggs. I was told she was their driving force to successed. The Panther salutes Mrs. Mattie Griggs for a job well done.

What happens to a soul when every door closes?

That's the question that confronted me at the death of my grandfather.

Since he had been my greatest source of encouragement and validation, I was left without my life mentor and best friend. Although I had long ago begun assisting mom and my siblings with family and school necessities, I sensed the need to step up emotional support. Mom had sent my youngest sister to live with my middle sister in another city, so only the two youngest brothers were going to school at home.

The ability for my brothers to remain home and attend school changed because by 1965, the school had decided to finally integrate following the 1954 Brown vs Board of Education decision by the supreme court. Although it was 1965 and 11 years after the decision, this was not a popular decision in southern Missouri.

The discipline codes for students were often not equally enforced meaning several Black students spent many days out on suspension for minor infractions. Rather than go to school under these conditions, my brother (five years younger),decided to quit high school. This caused my mom to send him to stay with me in Chicago so he could finish school. Many students made the same decision or dropped out altogether.

According to a 1966 Study Action Manual on Affluence and Poverty, a Manhattan neighborhood where 80% of young people(16-18) found it impossible to find employment, turned to all forms of death and despair such as drugs, alcohol, illigitimate relationships, and crime. Blacks faced limited opportunities for education, employment, and those who do work are concentrated in blue collar (41.9 Black/36.4 white), service (31.4 black/ 10.8 white) farm (8.3 black/ 6.3 white) or unemployed (9% black/4.3 white). In many cases membership in professional organizations, internships and unions are restricted or forbidden. This all leads to responding gaps in income and lifestyle for families. The saddest part of this is that it remains virtually unchanged for these groups in 2023. Arguably, today more black families are taking advantage of opportunities for upward mobility making use of junior colleges, job traning, etc. Progress is slowing in the face of the recent court decision to ban Affirmative Action in educational institutions, and the suspension of President Biden's plan for repayment of student college loans meant to encourage continued progress.

Further actions are being taken to discourage upward mobility among our poorest students. Some states are baning efforts to teach students their history, interferring with voting rights by passing anti voting legislation, prohibition, intimidation, threats, or terrorizing various groups forcing govermental intervention. Civil rights organizations such as the NAACP, ACLU, Southern Poverty Law Center and the Urban League are stepping up efforts to enforce legislation and encourage fairness and equity.

The simple fact is that in today's world, work generally done by the unskilled worker and by those with less than a high school education is being done by machines because it can be done cheaper. The heart of the racial descrimination problems today is the fact of lack of education and lack of work opportunity for those without education. Some even believe that the unemployed don't want to work, or are incapable of working. It is not a problem of not wanting, but a problem of not being prepared to work. Meanwhile many jobs go wanting because many are not trained. The mandate is clearly to answer the call for more training, education, internships as much as possible so as to pull oneself out of poverty. **The need is for justice and equity not charity.** Justice demands searching for solutions. These stories are born out everyday in urban and rural communities across America. Meanwhile many never venture out to find trade schools, community colleges, or internships available so these jobs go wanting.

Years of systemic racism have forced many in older generations to face these problems, but they have gone on and overcome segregation,homelessness, drug abuse, teenage pregnancy, without becoming overwhelmed; instead they took advice of mentors and ancestors to move beyond their problems. WHAT IS THE DIFFERENCE really IF 2 PEOPLE ARE KILLED BY BULLETS OR 2 PEOPLE DIE BECAUSE THEY ARE FORCED INTO A LIFE OF SQUALOR AND POVERTY AND LACK OF OPPORTUNITY BECAUSE OF THE COLOR OF THEIR SKIN?

Great advances were made through enormous hardship to leave a path for others who follow. Martin L. King, Jr. fought for (equality of man), while John Lewis fought for (voting rights), and many more gave their lives for the equality of future generations. Since we live in an age and time when fairness does not govern life nor death, groups like Southern Poverty

Law Center guards against hate groups, states rights, and any organization seeking to deny civil rights or equity for all. Democracy is an ongoing battle that every generation has to fight.

In the face of all that goes on to stagnate, discourage, destroy, and prevent progress for minorities, my family managed to graduate 6 out of 6 children with at least an Associates, ranging from teachers, and lawyer, to the Mayor of our small town. Progress is being made even in the face of court ruling reversals and changing educational standards. In St. Louis, the Black Pages is printed annually and seeks to highlight black businesses and inspire its readers. For the last several years its publisher has added an annual transformational workshop intended to help attendees look at their life's options and transform. **Today there are no excuses.** No one can truly say or believe that there are no options for them. Many groups and organizations are working digilently to open doors for you. YOU JUST HAVE TO WALK THROUGH. One thing we as a people must remember is that we can't be treated equal, if we want to be treated special.

WHAT CAN WE DO TO HELP FIGHT AGAINST HATE AND RACISM?

1. Embrace diversity as a strength along with others who share a commitment to justice and human rights.
2. Stay active in your local community. Speak out about your commitment to racial justice.
3. Support causes which work to defeat hate.
4. Arm yourself with the best available in education, job training, and relationships that you can possibly attain.
5. Lean in and adopt church and family virtues and values to sustain you in critical times.
6. Continue to learn and apply lessons and values of culture and history.
7. Be resolute and constant to all that enhances your fight for justice and equity for everyone.
8. Feed your soul with a steady diet of God's provision for you.
9. Meditate on God's word for it feeds your soul. Prov.1:1
10. Forgive others, Eph.4:26-27, 30-32.This is your best course in order to live in peace. **Leave room for God's justice.**

WE LIVE IN THE HOUSE WE BUILD

First and most important in my life has been the certainty and gravity of the grace of God.

My life story highlights actual events from my earliest memories (age 4) until well into my marriage of 62 years and life's work as a teacher, librarian, counselor, mother and Christian. Just like any other Black American living in America my life has been impacted by racism.

Racism is that belief that one race is superior to others.

Times and circumstances influence a life, but family, relationships and God preserves us no matter what else is going on in our world. My entire life has been affected by separate but equal laws (segregation, Jim Crow), and systemic racism which modifies and defines my life to this day. It's found in the highest levels of government, academia, medicine, judicial, business and even the religious world. As I look back I can remember stories of family, friends, colleagues' experiences which exemplify degrees of open hostility and retribution affecting evaluations and promotions which determined one's ability to be successful and even do one's job. Often subjective observations (hair styles, clothing, appearance, speech) having nothing to do with competance or credentials determine mobility. Using these criteria some have been denied opportunity or promotion, thus affecting salary and lifestyle.

I remember well the days of segregation where I was forced to walk to school, attend classes in rooms (sometimes containing 2 different grades) using books that had been thrown away by the other school, schools without plumbing, gyms, lunch rooms or libraries. I remember not being able to go to public parks, swimming pools, libraries or restaurants. But I also remember making a vow to change my life and set out to change it, even if I had to leave home. Gal. 3:26-28 is written to help assure us that Christ came to tear down walls between people, "You are all sons of God through faith in Christ Jesus. For all of you who were baptized into Christ have clothed yourself with Christ. There is neither Jew nor Greek, slave nor free, male nor female, for you are all one in Christ Jesus."

Racism is not new, nor is America the first place to practice racism. In early Bible history prejudice reared its ugly head. In Gen. 43:32 we find, "They (the Egyptian servants) served him (Joseph) by himself, the brothers by themselves, and the Egyptians who ate with him by themselves because Egypt could not eat with Hebrews, for that is detestable to Egyptians." Despite Joseph's high rank he still fell victim to prejudice, "They (Egyptian servants) would not eat at the same table with a Hebrew."

Although racism has influenced every facet of my life from birth to today (age 82), it is recognized simply as an evil force, not as the definition of who I am or hope to be. On the show,"Britian's Got Talent" a young man, Musa Motha (a dancer with one leg) from South Africa, in detailing his circumstances which led to the amputation of his leg, said," I define impossible, as I AM POSSIBLE". That's how I feel about my life's circumstances. I AM POSSIBLE, simply because of my world wide view of God. It says to me that Yes, I Can…ACHIEVE, BECOME, ACCOMPLISH, anything because with God I AM POSSIBLE; therefore nothing shall be impossible for me.

I can take this position and live by it because of my faith in God. THIS IS NOT A WHIMPY GOD. This is the same God who created heaven and earth and everything that is in it in 7 days. This is a God who does not change, The God of David, Moses, and our Lord, Jesus Christ. My faith has taught me that I am a collaborator in creation, as I do my part to become the person God has made me to be. I am possible because I insist on believing God's view of me. I ignore perceptions held by others or forces willingly ignorant of my abilities or insisting that I fit their mold. Instead, I search out God's view and persist in that.

In my house; my being, my self image, I see one who was designed by God; my mind, my intellect, my personality, my potential-all designed by a holy God, my creator. In Him I live, I move, I have my very being. To Him alone I owe allegiance. As I view the circumstances of my life being born American, Black, female and poor. I've worked on developing every facet of my life, every opportunity, stage, encounter into a productive moment.

Scripture tells us that God is a faithful partner and master. He faithfully protects, fights for, comforts, supports, consoles His people. Reading the Prophets Nahum and Habakkuk teach me that I can rely on Him just as His people always have. I don't waste my time hating.

Hating is a harm we do to ourselves. The book of Nahum is written to assure us that God is a God of justice. We often become weary thinking that wrongs done to us will never be vindicated. But in reading Nahum we are convinced and comforted when we understand the lengths to which God will go to vindicate His people. "Vengeance is mine says the Lord." Rom. 12:19. The desire for vengeance is human, but the Christian must live by faith. He must believe that God will rectify, make all things right. Nineveh was destroyed because it was a" bloody city, full of lies and pillage. Its people were guilty of harlotries, sorceries and enslaving nations," Nahum 3:4-7. The nature of God demands justice, Nahum1:2-6. The Lord is slow to anger but eventually He will destroy the wicked. Justice is evident in God's actions:

1. After the flood, God said,"who ever sheds man's blood, by man his blood shall be shed". Gen.9:6.
2. The Law of Moses required punishment for breaking the Law.
3. The New Testament endorses government's rights to punish wrong doers. Rom. 13:1-5.

For vengeance:

1. Wait on God, Nahum 3:16.
2. Remain faithful, no matter what. Rom. 13:1-5.
3. Find strength in the Lord Nahum 3:19 THE RIGHTEOUS WILL LIVE BY FAITH, Rom. 1:17, Gal.3:11, Heb.10:38, 39.
4. Nahum reminds us that those who live with injustice and evil will be vindicated

Habakkuk means to embrace, comprehend, enfold, clasp to the heart. The message is that those who are faithful to God through hard times-even if they have to experience trouble or suffer, will live. They will be blessed by God. In the face of so much suffering; injustice, violence, and evil, Habakkuk, like us, complained to God; "Why do you tolerate wrong?" 1:3 and "Why do you tolerate the treacherous? Why are you silent while the wicked swallow up the more righteous than themselves?" 1:13. God answers in 2:3-4, "Though it linger, it will certainly come. The righteous will live by faith."

God will repay. Habakkuk remains faithful and concludes, "I will wait patiently for the day of calamity to come on the nation invading us."

"Though the fig tree does not bud and there are no grapes on the vines, though the olive crop fails and the fields produce no food, though there are no sheep in the pen, and no cattle in the stalls, yet I will rejoice in the Lord, I will be joyful in God my savior." Hab. 3:17-18.

TRUST GOD, LEAVE ROOM FOR GOD'S WRATH. Remember, our willingness to wait reveals the value we place on what we are waiting for.

VICTORS NOT
VICTIMS

Pierre Teilhardde Chardin says it this way, "Our duty is to proceed as if limits to our abilities did not exist, We are collaborators in creation." I'm further convinced of this when I read from scripture, "FOR WE ARE GOD'S WORKMANSHIP, CREATED IN CHRIST JESUS TO DO GOOD WORKS, WHICH GOD PREPARED IN ADVANCE FOR US TO DO", Eph. 2:10.

Christianity demands that we act to help ourselves as well as help our neighbor. The question of neighbor comes up in Luke 10:29-37. The story of The GOOD SAMARITAN is told in answer to a young man's question to Jesus. The young lawyer wanted to know, "Who is my neighbor?" After the story the "expert in the law" correctly answered," A neighbor is the one who shows mercy". His answer rightly stated that a neighbor is one who answers a need for help, he gets involved, he shows mercy. He, and we, are told to go and do "likewise", go and help as we can, go and show mercy when we can. We are the neighbor when we answer the call for help, when we reach out and show mercy. Maybe we know of a job, or a scholarship source; we may be able to tutor someone in Math, or suggest a source of help. Whatever we can do to make it possible for someone else, we must go and do likewise. Our community is strengthened when we reach out. Each one, Teach one - reach out to one. That expresses the philosophy of my family. In growing up I remember well how my mom would reach out to neighbors during their trials. After the death of a parent, my mom would act as surrogate. The children often came to our house to share meals, get help with school, or just to be encouraged. All families shared food from their gardens. Grandpa and my dad often transported people to church or to shop. This is how we managed our resources, this was the strength of our community. Reaching out, helping, sharing; THIS IS THE TRUE PATH TO COLLABORATION. This is the good work scripture teaches us to do.

As parents of three children, my husband and I also followed this parenting guide. We taught our children to live a life according to the "good neighbor" model by which we were raised. Each one help one to build a stronger family, stronger community, stronger family of God.

Whatever your path, whatever your experience, don't waste it, grow from it. Practice overcoming by claiming your opportunities and turning them into victories. We must continue to overcome whatever obstacles are placed in our path, by being the change we want to see. Every person has the power to be the person he wants to be. But you must be willing to transform your self. Don't look to someone else to fix you. With your eyes firmly fixed upon your goal move steadily to complete it. It takes time, yes; energy, yes, money, yes. Whatever the cost we must be willing to pay it. Make the choice to transform yourself. BE A VICTOR, NOT A VICTIM!

AT 19, I made the choice to get married to my high school sweetheart. Since I had left home at graduation to go to Lincoln University in Jefferson City, Missouri on a scholarship, that meant having to give up my scholarship if I left Lincoln. At the time my husband (to be) lived and worked in Chicago.

Tough decision…moving to Chicago, giving up my scholarship; it could have spelled disaster, but I knew I couldn't disappoint mama. At the end of the first semester of my 2nd year at Lincoln I decided to move to Chicago. The first thing I did was look into schools, the cost, majors, location, travel. When these decisions were made I immediately applied and had my transcript sent. I then went about saving money for tuition since I had lost my schlorship. I found a job and saved every penny for the first semester cost. I was ready on registration day with my full tuition saved. What a shock, I went from free tuition to $30.00 per hour. I could only afford 9 hours that first semester so I decided to go to classes year round so as to graduate on time with my class. This decision meant that I would have to redouble all my efforts; work to pay my tuition, and take at least 12-15 hours at a time. When my 1959 class graduated in spring 1963, I was 1 semester behind them, graduating in December 1963. There were other painful choices I had to make: I remember leaving home every morning at about 6:30 for classes which began at 8. At about 4p.m. I left school on my way to my job at the Post Office where I worked until 10:00p.m.

I usually arrived home about 10:30 p.m. where I studied until about 1:00 a.m. and slept until 5:30 a.m. then started my day. Was the sacrifice worth it? Did I get tired and weary…did I want to give up? Yes. Yes, many days I wondered if I had made the right choice, but I never quit. I stayed the course and I met my goal.

The Transformational Workshop, created by Mr. Henson, publisher of the Black Pages is a yearly workshop set up to help you, me or any one who desires to transform his thinking, or life. The statement on the cover of the magazine says, "Remember, covenant was made with you hundreds of years ago. Your ancestors chose life, so that you might live free.

They endured hardships, so that you could know today! Knowing, trusting, believing that if they were strong enough to endure, you would one day return dignity, nobility, and joy to our people. Your time is now! Live lives of joy, and love, and positive accomplishment, of high character, the highest virtue, and exceptional values. It's in your genes; it's the essence of who you are. Empower yourselves with love. Create a healing community of love and you will thrive beyond your wildest dreams."

Copied from The Transformational Agenda magazine, p.48, 27th edition, 2022.

Remember, You were created to do good things. Let it begin with you!

Change your thoughts, from can't to can, from impossible to I am possible.

*YES, YOU CAN CHANGE YOUR THOUGHTS
AND CHANGE YOUR LIFE.*

VICTORS DO IT EVERY DAY!!!!

EPILOGUE

COLLABORATORS IN CREATION

"Our duty is to proceed as if limits to our ability did not exist. We are collaborators in creation". Pierre Teilhard de Chardin

This quote speaks to me. It says that we as Christians work in collaboration with God as we work to become the person He made us to be. It's in perfect alignment with Eph. 2:10 which states," For we are God's workmanship, created in Christ Jesus to do good works, which God prepared in advance for us to do."

We are indeed victors not victims as we fight the good fight for equal access to education, jobs, adequate housing, voting rights and civil rights for all. Victors are those who defeat the adversary, the winner in the fight for equity and justice. A victor overcomes the struggle, harm or suffering inflicted by another; be it persons, societies or governments.

Victors use their God given powers, sustained and strengthened by God to overcome and defeat the adversary. It's the story of good over evil, strength over weakness, determination over resignation.

Victors ground themselves in God's sovereignty, leaning upon His care for His creation. They lean, they learn, and they overcome.